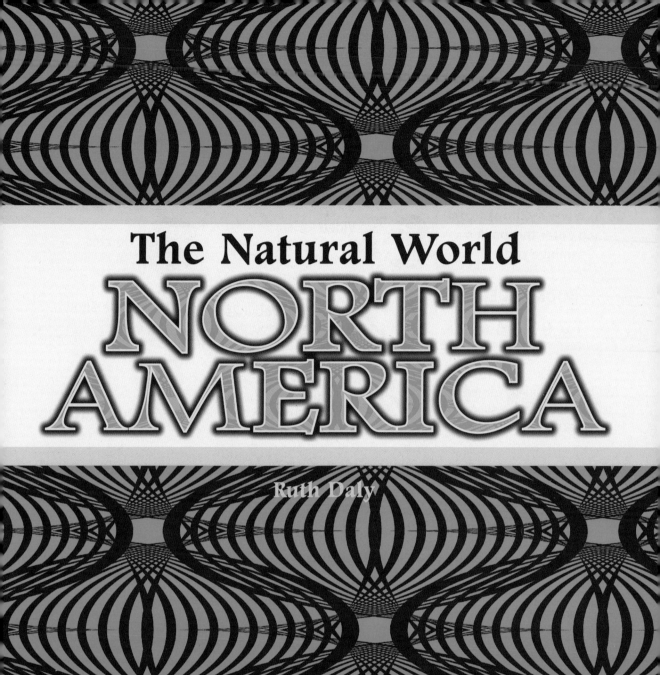

The Natural World
NORTH AMERICA

Ruth Daly

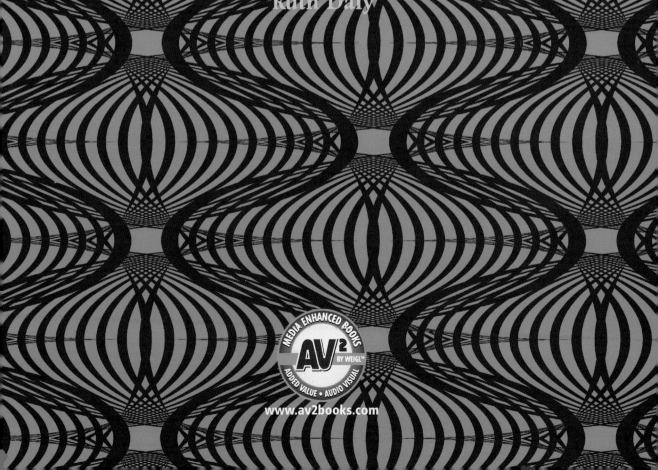

www.av2books.com

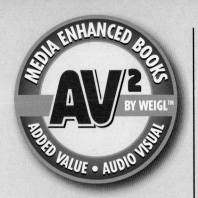

AV² provides enriched content that supplements and complements this book. Weigl's AV² books strive to create inspired learning and engage young minds in a total learning experience.

Your AV² Media Enhanced books come alive with...

Audio
Listen to sections of the book read aloud.

Key Words
Study vocabulary, and complete a matching word activity.

Video
Watch informative video clips.

Quizzes
Test your knowledge.

Embedded Weblinks
Gain additional information for research.

Slide Show
View images and captions, and prepare a presentation.

Try This!
Complete activities and hands-on experiments.

... and much, much more!

Go to **www.av2books.com**, and enter this book's unique code.

BOOK CODE

T 7 9 3 6 4 4

AV² by Weigl brings you media enhanced books that support active learning.

Published by AV² by Weigl
350 5th Avenue, 59th Floor
New York, NY 10118
Websites: www.av2books.com   www.weigl.com

Library of Congress Cataloging-in-Publication Data
Daly, Ruth, 1962- author.
 North America / Ruth Daly.
    pages cm. -- (The natural world)
 Summary: "North America extends from the Arctic regions of Canada and Greenland to the deserts of Mexico and countries of Central America. The landscape of North America ranges from grasslands to deserts. Learn more about this exciting environment in North America. This is an AV2 media enhanced book. A unique book code printed on page 2 unlocks multimedia content. This book comes alive with video, audio, weblinks, slide shows, activities, hands-on experiments, and much more."-- Provided by publisher.
 Includes index.
 ISBN 978-1-4896-0954-0 (hardcover : alk. paper) -- ISBN 978-1-4896-0955-7 (softcover : alk. paper) --
ISBN 978-1-4896-0956-4 (single user ebk.) -- ISBN 978-1-4896-0957-1 (multi user ebk.)
 1. Natural history--North America--Juvenile literature. 2. Ecology--North America--Juvenile literature. 3. North America--Environmental conditions--Juvenile literature. I. Title.
 QH102.D35 2015
 578.097--dc23
                        2014004674

Printed in the United States of America in North Mankato, Minnesota
1 2 3 4 5 6 7 8 9 0 18 17 16 15 14

042014
WEP150314

Editor: Heather Kissock
Design: Mandy Christiansen

Weigl acknowledges Getty Images as its primary image supplier for this title.

Contents

Welcome to North America!

North America, the third largest continent in the world, covers an area of more than 9,540,198 square miles (24,708,999 square kilometers). Many diverse landscapes are found across the continent, such as mountains, tundra, and deserts. The largest region in North America is grassland, which covers an area of about 1.4 million square miles (3,625,983 sq. km). It is known as the "breadbasket" because of the large amount of grain grown there. The second largest **coral reef** in the world is located in the Caribbean Sea, which is south of the mainland. There are four main deserts in North America. Together, they take up between 500,000 and 730,000 square miles (1,294,994 and 1,890,691 sq. km).

Each region is home to a wide variety of plant and animal life. Bears can be found in the tundra and forest regions. Snakes and spiders inhabit the deserts, while grasshoppers and coyotes can be found in the grasslands. North America has more than 90,000 **species** of insects, 482 species of mammals, and about 900 species of birds. North America is unique from other continents because of its diversity of landforms, plants, and animals.

Approximately **19,000** types of flowering plants are found in North America.

The Gila monster is one of the only poisonous lizards in North America.

Pronghorns are one of the fastest animals in North America and can run up to 40 miles (65 km) per hour.

The only marsupial that lives in North America is the common opossum.

Bald eagles can be found along North America's seacoasts, beside lakes and rivers, and even in swamplands.

Unique North American Life

Many kinds of plants, mammals, insects, reptiles, and birds are found across the North American continent. Among these, some are native to North America and cannot be found anywhere else. Species that are found only in a particular region are called endemic. Pronghorn sheep, bald eagles, and wild turkeys are examples of species endemic to North America. Some endemic species, such as the California condor, live only in one particular region of North America.

The Caribbean region consists of about 7,000 islands, reefs, and cays in the warm waters of the Caribbean Sea. The climate and landforms of this region vary, ranging from **rainforests** to coral reefs. Several plant and animal species that inhabit the islands and their waters cannot be found anywhere else in the world. Brightly colored fish, sea turtles, and sea horses are among the creatures that live in these waters.

The northern spotted owl is endemic to the west coast of the continent. It can be found living in old-growth forests from British Columbia to California.

The Caribbean

Florida

Caribbean

The Caribbean region has about 10 square miles (26,000 sq. km) of coral reef.

The Barbados threadsnake is the world's smallest snake.

Approximately 60 species of hard coral are found in the Caribbean region.

The Caribbean region has between 500 and 700 species of fish.

94% of the reptile species in the Caribbean are endemic.

The Caribbean is home to about 160 endemic bird species.

The Aruba island rattlesnake is the most endangered rattlesnake in the world.

Of the Caribbean's 13,000 plant species, 50% are endemic.

Where in the World?

North America is located in the northern hemisphere and is bordered on three sides by the Pacific, Atlantic, and Arctic Oceans. The continent extends from the Arctic regions of Canada and Greenland in the north to the hot deserts of Mexico and the countries of Central America in the south. It is connected to South America by a narrow bridge of land. The continent also includes the small islands of the Caribbean Sea. The varied temperatures and rainfall levels determine the types of plant and animal life in North America.

One factor affecting the climate of a region is its distance from the **equator**. Countries in the southern part of North America are warmer because they are close to the equator. The northern parts of the continent are colder because they are far from the equator.

ASIA

ARCTIC OCEAN

EUROPE

PACIFIC OCEAN

NORTH AMERICA

ATLANTIC OCEAN

SOUTH AMERICA

EQUATOR

North American Biomes

Geographical regions that have similar climates are called biomes. Although similar biomes are found throughout the world, the types of plants and animals found on different continents vary. North America has several biomes, including chaparral, grassland, forest, desert, and tundra.

The Chihuahuan Desert is one of North America's four main deserts. It is located in the southern part of the continent, mostly in Mexico.

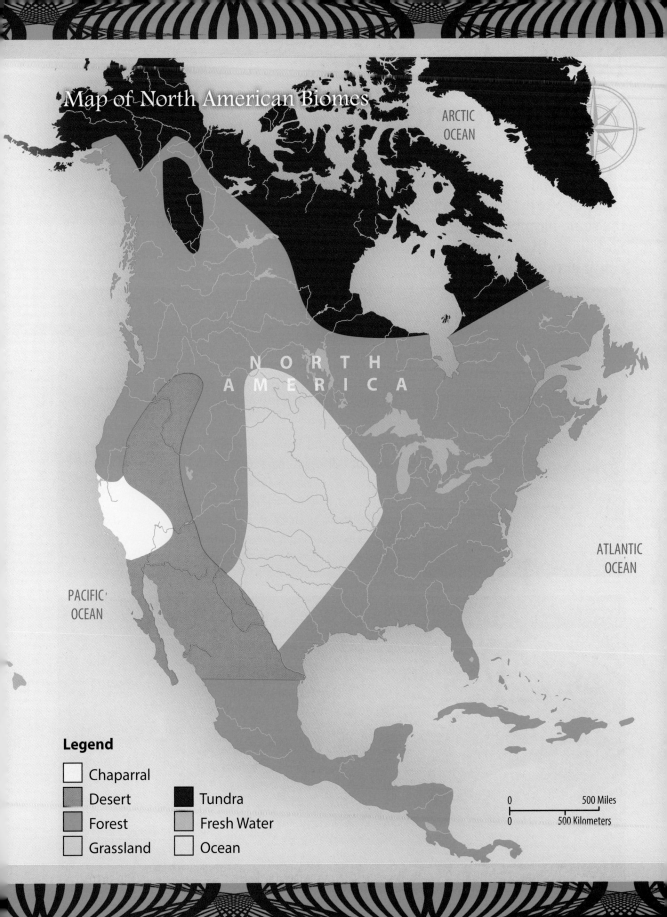

Map of North American Biomes

ARCTIC OCEAN

N O R T H
A M E R I C A

ATLANTIC OCEAN

PACIFIC OCEAN

Legend

- Chaparral
- Desert
- Forest
- Grassland
- Tundra
- Fresh Water
- Ocean

0   500 Miles
0   500 Kilometers

North American Land Biomes

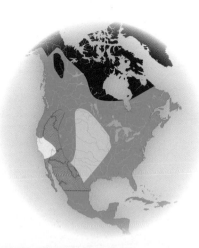

Each type of biome has a different set of characteristics. The four major biomes of North America all have similar climates to the same biomes on other continents. The animals and plants that live in the same biomes on different continents also have similarities.

Grassland

In North America, grasslands are called prairies or plains. Prairie grassland covers most of central North America.

Plants: Grasses in this biome, such as big bluestem and Indian grass, have deep roots to reach water in dry conditions. Flowers in the biome include milkweed and fleabane.

Animals: Deer, elk, and bison are some of the **herbivores** living in the grasslands. Burrowing animals, such as prairie dogs, can also be found.

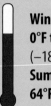

Winter
0°F to 50°F
(−18 to 10°C)
Summer
64°F to 82°F
(18 to 28°C)

Rainfall
12 to 24"
(31 to 61 cm)

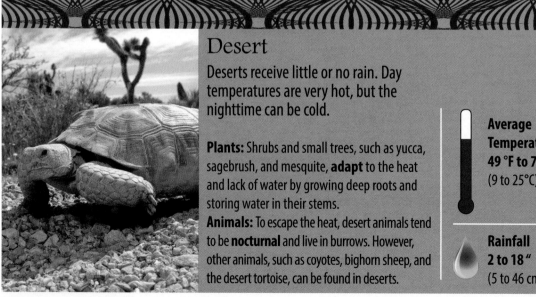

Desert

Deserts receive little or no rain. Day temperatures are very hot, but the nighttime can be cold.

Plants: Shrubs and small trees, such as yucca, sagebrush, and mesquite, **adapt** to the heat and lack of water by growing deep roots and storing water in their stems.

Animals: To escape the heat, desert animals tend to be **nocturnal** and live in burrows. However, other animals, such as coyotes, bighorn sheep, and the desert tortoise, can be found in deserts.

Average Temperature:
49 °F to 77 °F
(9 to 25°C)

Rainfall
2 to 18 "
(5 to 46 cm)

The exact species that live in a biome are different for each continent and region within the continent. For example, a desert biome is home to lizards that can live in dry heat. However, the lizard species that live in the Great Basin Desert of Arizona and Colorado may be different from those that live in the Chihuahuan Desert farther south.

Forest

North America has three types of forests. These are coniferous, deciduous, and rainforests. Most forests in North America have warm summers and cool winters.

Plants: Pine, fir, evergreen trees, oak trees, maples, dogwood, mosses, and ferns grow in this biome.
Animals: Mammals that live in forests include raccoons, red foxes, white-tailed deer, squirrels, black bears, marmots, wolverines, and lynx.

Average Temperature 50°F (10°C)

Rainfall 12 to 24" (31 to 61 cm)

Tundra

This treeless region has freezing temperatures and frozen soil. Plants and animals are adapted to the harsh climate.

Plants: Many types of mosses, lichens, and **algae** grow in the tundra.
Animals: Some tundra animals, such as bears, **hibernate** during the winter. Birds, such as the ptarmigan, remain year round, while others, such as the Arctic tern, **migrate**.

Winter −30° to −20°F (−34 to −29°C)
Summer 37 to 60°F (3 to 16°C)

Rainfall 12 to 20" (31 to 51 cm)

North American Ecosystems and Habitats

Within a biome, there are many different ecosystems. Ecosystems are groups of living organisms, such as plants and animals, that exist in the same environment. The organisms interact and depend on each other for food, shelter, and many other aspects of life. An ecosystem can be a large expanse of land, such as a forest, or it can be as small as a tree or pond.

The place in which a plant or animal lives is called its habitat. A habitat provides the things that are necessary for life, such as oxygen, food, water, and an appropriate temperature for survival.

The Great Plains are the grassland region between the Rocky Mountains and the state of Indiana. Burrowing animals such as gophers, rabbits, and prairie dogs inhabit these lands. Insects, such as grasshoppers, can become an issue when large numbers destroy crops.

The majority of North America's desert land stretches north to south, from Oregon to northern Mexico.

The Mojave Desert is the smallest desert in North America. Plants are scarce. Among the most common are creosote bushes and Joshua trees. Several species of birds nest in Joshua trees.

Hawai'ian honeycreepers are small birds that are endemic to the rainforests of Hawai'i. Their beaks are adapted for eating the kinds of insects, nectar, fruits, and seeds that grow in the honeycreeper's rainforest habitat.

Tundra plants have adapted to the harsh temperatures and **permafrost**. Reindeer moss is a low, fast-growing lichen that only grows to about six inches (15 cm) high.

The smallest bat in North America is the western pipistrelle. It lives in the Mojave Desert.

Plant Life in North America

Plants in North America have adapted certain features that enable them to survive in their specific habitats. Plants that need very little water can live in the hot, dry desert regions. Grassland vegetation is adapted to limited rainfall, seasonal droughts, and fires. In the tundra, plants survive freezing temperatures and frozen ground. The plant species found in forests form layers of vegetation and are adapted to grow to a certain height. Plants in the **canopy** have different features from those growing on the ground.

The purple saxifrage is one of the first tundra plants to bloom in the spring.

Purple Saxifrage

The purple saxifrage belongs to a group of tundra plants known as "cushion plants." They are called this because they grow in small clumps and look like cushions. The purple saxifrage grows on rocky ground and forms a tight clump to protect itself from cold winds. Tiny hairs found on its leaves capture heat.

Indian Grass

Indian grass grows up to 8 feet (2.4 m) high on the grasslands of Canada and the United States. It has wide, blue-green leaves, large feathery seed heads, and golden yellow flowers. Indian grass is able to grow in both sunny and shady conditions and in many types of soils.

Indian grass produces beautiful plume-like flowers. Its seeds are food for birds and small mammals living on the prairie.

Orchid

Orchids belong to a group of plants called **epiphytes**. They live on the tree branches in the rainforest. Orchids get their nutrients from the rain and from organisms that fall from the branches and leaves above them.

Orchids grow in tropical climates. Certain species are used in the production of vanilla.

Saguaro Cactus

The saguaro cactus grows in the Sonoran Desert. It stores water in its pleated stem, which is able to expand. Its root system collects and stores rainwater, which keeps the plant alive. Under the right conditions, a saguaro cactus can live up to 200 years.

The saguaro cactus grows its branches, or arms, when it reaches between 15 and 25 feet (4.6 and 7.6 m).

Just the Facts

The Caribbean National Forest in Puerto Rico has **225** species of native trees.

The dahlia is the national flower of Mexico.

Of the many orchid species found in Hawai'i, only three are native to the area.

The saguaro cactus is the largest cactus in the United States.

Mesquite plants have taproots that grow to depths of **30** feet (9 m).

Insects, Reptiles, and Amphibians

Crickets, mosquitoes, wasps, and houseflies are some of the many insects in North America. They are food for many reptiles and amphibians. Lizards, frogs, snakes, and tortoises can be found in various wilderness areas of the continent. Many of these insects, reptiles, and amphibians have unique features that help them to survive in their different ecosystems.

Male crickets use their wings to make a chirping sound that attracts mates.

Crickets

Crickets are about 1 inch (2.54 cm) long, with large legs for jumping. Their eyes are adapted to see in several different directions at once. Crickets are a main food source for many creatures, including spiders, birds, reptiles, and small mammals. To avoid these **predators**, crickets stay hidden under rocks and logs during the day.

Sidewinder Snake

The sidewinder adapts to the desert climate by being active mainly at night. By day, it finds shelter in burrows made by other animals. It is called sidewinder because of the way it travels across the ground. Only two sections of its body come into contact with the hot sand at any time.

Sidewinder snakes leave trails of J-shaped markings behind them in the sand.

Spring Peeper

The spring peeper is one of North America's most common frogs. Although peepers can be tan, gray, or dark green, all spring peepers have a distinctive "X" on their backs. Large, sticky pads on their toes help them to climb trees and bushes. They live in wooded areas close to water, which they need in order to mate and lay their eggs.

A spring peeper frog can jump more than 17 times the length of its body. This allows it to easily catch the flying insects that make up its diet.

Bolson Tortoise

The Bolson tortoise has front legs with heavy, flat claws that it uses for digging burrows in the desert sand. This tortoise is adapted to the temperatures of the hot Chihuahuan Desert. It feeds early in the morning and in the evening when it is cooler. The tortoise stays in its burrow during the day. The Bolson tortoise hibernates during the winter.

The life span of a Bolson tortoise ranges from 80 to 100 years.

Just the Facts

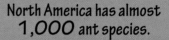

There are about **2,500** spider species in North America.

North America has almost *1,000* ant species.

The largest spider in the North American desert is the desert tarantula. Its leg span is between 6 and 7 inches (15 and 18 cm).

The giant swallowtail is the largest North American butterfly. Its wingspan measures 4 to 6 inches (10 to 15 cm).

About **350** species of amphibians are found in North America.

Birds and Mammals

Just as the landscapes in North America are diverse, so are the mammals and birds that inhabit each region. Some mammals are considered dangerous, such as grizzly bears and cougars. Others, such as rodents and raccoons, are considered pests. Although North America has a large landmass, there is less diversity among mammals than some other continents. Mexico, with 500 species of mammals, has the most variety of all North American countries. North America has some of the world's most colorful birds.

Small hummingbirds can beat their wings more than 70 times per second. Larger birds beat their wings at a slower rate.

Hummingbirds

Hummingbirds are the smallest birds in North America. They are named for the sound their wings make when beating. Hummingbirds live in several biomes, including the tundra, forest, and grassland. Important food sources for hummingbirds are insects and nectar, which they reach using their long bills and tongues.

American Bison

Found in pockets throughout the North American grasslands, the bison is the largest land-dwelling mammal in North America. Males can grow to almost 10 feet (3 m) tall and weigh more than 1 ton (907 kg). Bison are grazing animals, living off the grasses and plants in the area. They live in herds that vary in size from a family unit to several hundred.

Bison can run at speeds up to 32 miles (51.5 km) per hour. They will stampede at these speeds when frightened.

Black Bear

The black bear is North America's most common bear. It can be found in forest, mountain, and grassland areas. Black bears eat berries, nuts, honey, fish, small mammals, and **carrion**. They are mainly active at night, and they hibernate during winter.

Black bears have a good sense of smell but poor eyesight and hearing.

Rock Ptarmigan

The rock ptarmigan lives on the ground in the tundra regions. Its color changes seasonally to blend in with the environment. In winter, its feathers turn white so it is hidden by the snow. In the short summers, the ptarmigan has a mottled appearance so it can blend easily with the forest.

Rock ptarmigans are prey for other birds and animals such as the snowy owl and arctic fox.

30% of a hummingbird's body weight comes from its flight muscles.

The antlers of the male moose are the largest of any animal in the world.

Prairie dogs DOUBLE their weight in summer.

The national bird of the United States is the bald eagle.

Arctic foxes can survive in temperatures as low as **−58°F** *(−50°C).*

North American Aquatic Biomes

I n addition to land biomes, aquatic biomes are also found in North America. They are classified as being freshwater or marine, depending on the concentration of salt in the water.

Aquatic Ecosystems and Habitats

There are many different ecosystems and habitats in aquatic biomes. Each one supports a variety of plant and animal life. The three oceans that surround North America make up most of its marine biome. Ocean ecosystems are defined by the amount of sunlight they receive, the temperature of the water, and its depth. These conditions determine which kinds of living things can survive within that ecosystem.

Marine Biome

Oceans form the largest part of North America's marine biome. Water closest to the surface of an ocean receives more sunlight than deeper areas. Coral reefs can be found in warm, shallow areas. The coral reef located off the coast of Belize, in Central America, is the second largest in the world.

Plants: Eelgrass, seaweed, and sea grass are some of the plants that grow in North America's marine biomes.

About 3% salt content

Animals: Mollusks, **plankton**, sandpipers, whales, and sharks make their home in the waters of marine biomes.

Large freshwater lakes can be found in the northern part of the continent. Lake Superior and Lake Huron are among the largest freshwater lakes in the world. The longest river in North America is the Missouri River. It flows into the Mississippi River which is the second longest river in the United States. Together, they form the Mississippi-Missouri river system, which is 3,740 miles (6,019 km) long.

Lake Superior is home to 38 native fish species, including lake trout and whitefish.

Freshwater Biome

North America's freshwater biome is made up of lakes, ponds, rivers, and wetlands. Different water conditions exist in each. Life in rivers depends on the speed in which the river flows and the amount of nutrients within the water. Water in small lakes and ponds does not usually flow. As a result, large amounts of nutrients are found in these small bodies of water. This allows large populations of tiny organisms to thrive.

Plants: Algae, reeds, water lilies, and cattails can be found growing in a freshwater biome.

Less than 1% salt content

Animals: The freshwater biome is home to dragonflies, salmon, mink, heron, and alligators.

North American Aquatic Life

Temperature, oxygen levels, and nutrients in the water affect the plants in freshwater and marine biomes. Algae are aquatic plants that produce food and oxygen. Like most plants, algae use the energy from the Sun to produce food. Different species of plants are adapted to live in salt water or fresh water. Fish species are also adapted to life in fresh or salt water. Birds, such as ducks and loons, and mammals, such as beavers and otters, live in freshwater lakes and estuaries. Marine mammals, such as seals, whales, and dolphins, live underwater but must surface in order to breathe.

Terns have pointed bills. They use their bills to pierce prey, such as herrings and crabs.

Terns

Terns can be found along coastal areas and near inland waters. They are agile birds that can dive into water and soar through the air. When terns migrate, their long pointed wings and tail feathers enable them to travel long distances. There are 17 known types of terns in North America.

The American Alligator

The American alligator lives in the marshes, rivers, and swamps of the southern United States. It is the largest reptile in North America. Males can grow to between 10 and 15 feet (3 and 4.6 m) in length and weigh up to 1,000 pounds (454 kg). Females are slightly smaller than males. As a predator, the alligator's diet consists mainly of the small mammals, snakes, and turtles that share its habitat.

An alligator will lay in the sunlight to keep warm. It cannot control its internal body temperature.

California Sea Lion

The California sea lion lives in cool ocean waters. It can swim up to 25 miles (40 km) per hour by moving its front flippers up and down like wings. California sea lions have four flippers that enable it to walk quickly on land. Sea lions feed mainly on fish and crustaceans. They swallow their food in large chunks without chewing it.

California sea lions have a thick layer of fat called blubber beneath the surface of their skin. This helps to keep their bodies warm in cold water.

Lake Trout

Lake trout are one of the largest freshwater fishes. They are found in the lakes and rivers of Canada and parts of the United States. Lake trout measure about 4 feet (1.2 m) in length and can be identified by the white spots on their head, back, tail, and fins. Fish, insects, crustaceans, and plankton form the main part of the lake trout's diet.

Lake trout prefer to live in cold, deep waters.

Just the Facts

The Belize coral reef contains **65** identified species of coral.

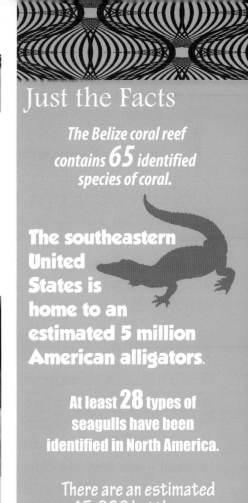

The southeastern United States is home to an estimated 5 million American alligators.

At least **28** types of seagulls have been identified in North America.

There are an estimated 45,000 bottlenose dolphins living in the northern waters of the Gulf of Mexico.

The United States has 3.5 million miles (5.6 million km) of rivers and approximately 100,000 lakes.

Maintaining Balance

In any ecosystem, the interaction of climate, plants, and animal life is important. The types of plants that grow in an ecosystem are a result of temperature and rainfall. Certain insects, reptiles, and amphibians are attracted to specific types of plants, which affects the kinds of mammals and birds that inhabit the area. This is why diversity is important in North America. When a continent has a variety of different ecosystems, it is possible for many different types of plants to grow. These plants attract and support a variety of herbivores, the food source for **carnivores**. A large diversity of species in an ecosystem keeps it in balance.

Introducing New Species

The balance in an ecosystem can be negatively impacted when a new species is introduced. When a new species enters an ecosystem, it does not usually have natural predators to keep the population under control. The population will often increase rapidly as there is nothing to keep the natural balance. Purple loosestrife was introduced in North America from Europe in the 1800s. This wetland plant can grow more quickly than the native species in the ecosystem. As it grows, it forms dense mats that choke other wetland plants. These two factors have reduced the populations of many native plant species. This, in turn has affected the animal populations. In

Purple loosestrife has damaged wetlands as far west as Alberta in western Canada, and as far east as New York State in the United States.

North America, purple loosestrife is not a food source for mammals, birds, fish, or insects. As the plant continued to spread, animals native to wetland areas moved away. Purple loosestrife also reduces, and in some cases destroys, habitats for fish and waterfowl.

Ecosystem Interactions

All living things in an ecosystem are connected. They are each part of a food chain. A food chain shows the transfer of energy from organism to organism. Plants are producers because they use the Sun's energy to make food. Primary consumers are the herbivores that eat plants. Secondary consumers are carnivores, which eat primary consumers. Decomposers break down dead organisms and put nutrients back into the soil for growing plants.

The Red-tailed Hawk
The red-tailed hawk is a secondary consumer. It eats many different types of animals, including mice and sidewinders.

Pocket Mouse
Pocket mice live near mesquite trees. They are primary consumers and use the trees as shelter from the desert heat and to hide from predators. The seeds from the mesquite tree provide a source of food and water for the pocket mouse.

The Sidewinder Snake
The sidewinder snake is a secondary consumer. It lives in animal burrows during the day to shelter it from the desert heat. Its diet includes pocket mice.

Nitrogen-fixing Bacteria
Nitrogen-fixing bacteria live in the taproot of the mesquite tree. As decomposers, they are part of the process by which nitrogen is restored to the soil.

The Mesquite Tree
The mesquite tree is a producer. It has small waxy leaves and a deep root that absorbs water from the soil. This root can reach to 200 feet (61 m) below the surface.

Diversity for Humans

Humans benefit from the diversity of North American ecosystems. Plants and animals have always been an important source of food, shelter, and medicine. Plants contain different vitamins and nutrients people need to live a healthy life. North America is known for its farmland and its cereal crops, such as wheat, oats, rice, and corn. These grains are important food sources from which many other foods are made. Grasslands are also important grazing lands for cattle, another important food source for humans.

Human Impact

The habitats of many North American species are threatened as the demand for land increases. To grow food, grasslands have been converted for agricultural use. In other cases, land has been cleared for building cities and roads. These actions destroy habitats and affect the animal populations within them. Food chains are affected, which creates an imbalance in the ecosystem. When habitats are completely destroyed, many of the species that depend on that habitat die as well.

Eastern meadowlark populations declined by 97 percent from 1966 to 1991 due to the conversion of grassland for farming use.

More than 30 percent of the world's corn is produced in the grasslands of the United States.

Conserving Nature

Many people are concerned about the **conservation** of North America's ecosystems, including those in government and various organizations. More than 181 million acres (73 million hectares) of land throughout North America have been set aside for national parks and preserves. Certain activities, such as land use and hunting, are strictly controlled in these protected areas. In some areas, native species have been reintroduced into their natural habitats.

When land and marine areas are protected, the organisms that live within those areas are protected, too. Plant and animal life can develop naturally. As the conservation of these areas continues, there is a greater possibility that some of North America's diverse life forms, endemic species, and unique landscapes can be preserved.

In 1996, biologists began reintroducing the California condor into the Grand Canyon. The birds had not been part of the park ecosystem for more than 70 years.

Make an Ecosystem Web

Use this book, and research on the Internet, to create a North American ecosystem.

1. Find a North American plant or animal. Think about the habitat in which it lives.
2. Find at least three organisms that are found in the same habitat. This could include plants, insects, amphibians, reptiles, birds, and mammals.
3. How do these species interact with each other? Do they provide food or shelter for the other organisms?
4. Begin linking these organisms together to show which organisms rely on each other for food or shelter.
5. Once your ecosystem web is complete, think about how removing one organism would affect the other organisms in the web.

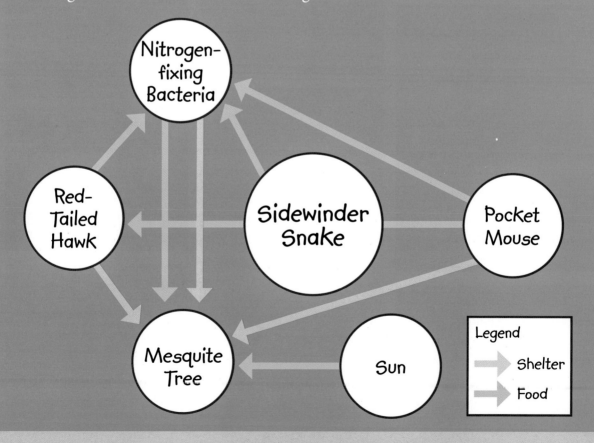

Quiz

1 What is the only marsupial found in North America?

The common opossum

2 What is the name for a species that is only found in one particular area?

Endemic

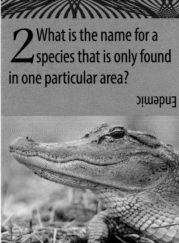

3 What are two factors that determine animal and plant life?

Temperature and rainfall

4 What are North America's grasslands sometimes called?

The breadbasket

5 Why are most desert animals nocturnal?

To escape the heat

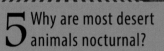

6 What is the name of North America's smallest desert?

Mojave Desert

7 Where are North America's coral reefs found?

In the Caribbean Sea off the coast of Belize.

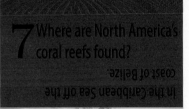

9 Which non-native species was introduced to North America in the 1800s, causing the destruction of wetland habitats?

Purple loosestrife

8 Name two of the largest freshwater lakes in the world.

Lake Superior and Lake Huron

10 Name the parts of the food chain.

Decomposer, producer, primary consumer, and secondary consumer

Key Words

adapt: to change to suit an environment

algae: organisms that produce oxygen

canopy: the top layer of a forest

carnivores: meat-eating animals

carrion: the remains of dead animals

conservation: protecting something from destruction

coral reef: underwater structures made up of calcium carbonate and populated by marine organisms

epiphytes: plants that do not come into contact with soil

equator: an imaginary line drawn across Earth's center

herbivores: plant-eating animals

hibernate: to spend the winter resting

migrate: to move with the seasons

nocturnal: primarily active at night

permafrost: a layer of soil that remains frozen all year

plankton: tiny organisms found in the ocean

predators: organisms that hunt other living things for food

rainforests: forests that receive large amounts of rain and have very tall trees

species: a group of animals or plants that share similar features

Index

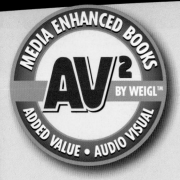

Log on to www.av2books.com

AV² by Weigl brings you media enhanced books that support active learning. Go to www.av2books.com, and enter the special code found on page 2 of this book. You will gain access to enriched and enhanced content that supplements and complements this book. Content includes video, audio, weblinks, quizzes, a slide show, and activities.

AV² Online Navigation

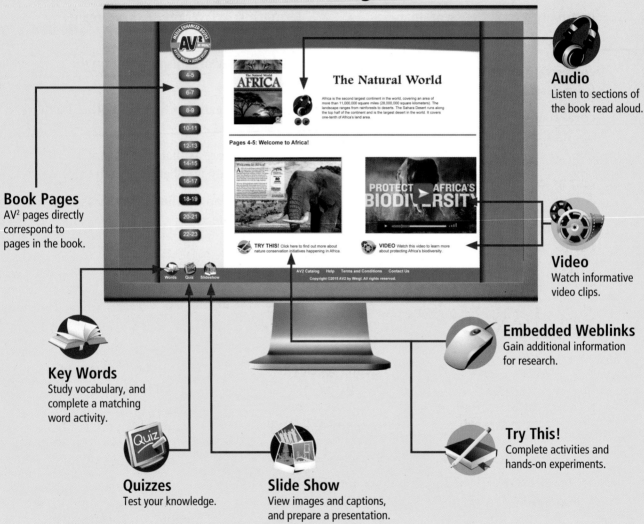

Audio
Listen to sections of the book read aloud.

Book Pages
AV² pages directly correspond to pages in the book.

Video
Watch informative video clips.

Key Words
Study vocabulary, and complete a matching word activity.

Embedded Weblinks
Gain additional information for research.

Quizzes
Test your knowledge.

Slide Show
View images and captions, and prepare a presentation.

Try This!
Complete activities and hands-on experiments.

AV² was built to bridge the gap between print and digital. We encourage you to tell us what you like and what you want to see in the future.

Sign up to be an AV² Ambassador at www.av2books.com/ambassador.

Due to the dynamic nature of the internet, some of the URLs and activities provided as part of AV² by Weigl may have changed or ceased to exist. AV² by Weigl accepts no responsibility for any such changes. All media enhanced books are regularly monitored to update addresses and sites in a timely manner. Contact AV² by Weigl at 1-866-649-3445 or av2books@weigl.com with any questions, comments, or feedback.